In Black Ill White

ISBN-13: 9781539545651

ISBN-10: 1539545652

Printed in the United States of America

In Black

Review the Past

Create a better future

Never lose
the passion to fight

# Death or a Slave

A Badge of Metal.

A Heart of Flesh.

A Gun of Steel.

A mind for the divide.

Bodies fueled by Hate.

Hate for us.

They are them.

We are us.

Abortion, housing gentrification, mass incarnation, dilapidated schools.

Lack of sexual literacy, dropout rates soar.

Parallel to the estimate of the number that the billions of dollars your private research has portrayed.

So they can profit on my chains.

Or I'm struggling by the hourly wage for slaves.

Never financially stable.

Cultivating us perfectly to never leave the Welfare stables.

The black of our skin is 60 years behind.

Evading statistics is another crime.

Going to college, and finally getting out of the waters and see a future tangible for me.

Is like screaming "racist" in the faces of the supporters of Donald Trump.

Offended and frustrated.

Uh oh, here the aggression comes.

It bundles and rumbles like Confederate flag attackers.

No matter my education,

The back lagging, laughers.

Will always have pitchforks and torches that bully my "Black Lives Matters".

Feelings turning sour.

Wishing we could turn back hours,

Revise our very steps.

Have votes count for something,

Not just a suggestion for superdelegates.

I wish I could be free.

Maybe if I was free,

I could breathe in this indoctrination of democracy.

Psh. I'm just trying to live pass my 20's.

Guess death was their definition of free.

Death or a Slave.

Principles of progress will never instate my name.

## Absent Leader

Pressing millions of my color out to my street to wonder.

Looting and rioting.

You are lucky we don't have a leader.

You are saved because we don't have a King or X to make you choose your every breath.

Make the way to work a little hard,

With swarms of people taking the highways as a voice.

Freeing my Mexican and Muslim brothers too.

It's the brotherhood of the colored

& your color is invited too.

Speak loud, Let your voice ring like cloud.

Let the earth shutter like the steps of an army advancing to the lines.

No more protesting, We wage a new war.

One that's can't be spoken but only heard...

# I Had A Dream...

I had a dream.

I woke up and I was on the hills,

But I was standing on the blood of the Indians.

Like a flood it rushed into the massacre of the innocence.

So many evil things have taken place in my Lord's name.

They destroyed generations,

People whose advancements allowed us to make it on this foreign land.

They give us berries,

We give them lead.

We shot all of them, as much as we can.

It was a sport for the whites to hunt people.

It wasn't immoral it was already a practice.

Since they captured slaves and equated darker pigmentation as lesser.

I sometimes wonder why God allowed me in this specific time period.

If I was just 200 years earlier I think havoc would've been created.

America would have had a Nate Turner for every plantation.

Burning chains,

Teaching change.

The history books would have a lighter note.

Dipped into the sorrow song, of the 300 years of slaves.

I would have FREED! EVERY individual with Tubman and raise the bounty to catch us by the millions.

We would've created cities where freed slaves could create business.

Black Wallstreet

That filled streets with colors melting them like toast on butter.

It was naive of us to think a people without color could embrace the world colored.

All I know is I seen kids play with other races with no discrimination,

Because the aspect of understanding was only joy, fun and apple juice.

Everyone was equal.

Children get acceptance more than professors, politicians and policemen.

I have a dream that we revert back into children.

Shedding the colors on paper from the crayon box.

Staying

within

the    lines    giving    each    its    plot.

## Milk Chocolate

I don't want to see a brother rep another color,

If they don't got a check coming from the Headquarters of Crayola.

Saying your doing a fine job blue,

Or Red, keep firing away you're boosting all our sells.

I need some help to see, why the crayon boxes more white than anything.

Speaking of diversity,

While universities still looks like 1850's.

But now, they have just enough of the minority,

That they can dot the last page of their funding.

Staying in the mirror,

Checking my age.

Cause even though the days have change,

The climate is still the same.

Racism has been the biggest terrorist threat we ever seen.

Pause ISIS.

We been refugees for centuries.

I could go to slavery,

But skip forward.

It's the fact we are just seeing all whites running the states.

While we keep getting pushed out our house for the new era of suburban race .

Relocation by raising rent, pressing more people of color to projects.

We been scared, we still scared.

They never cared.

They been safe, now it's threatened

They feel weird.

I always tried to reason,

But with thoughts trumping,

Even the elections show the cracks that we facing.

Minorities, they been blinding our eye , keeping us focused on one thing at a time.

Because if we connect dots of lies,

The docks in pay and how the prison and unemployment lines are always occupied by those who color resembles a darker shade.

They lock us up for moving snow,

Unless snow can have medical uses, and they already racked up millions of our brothers and sisters to be new slaves.

Then they will Wall Street it to make billions.

One day we will start dipping into the milk with dirty fingers,

Washing every nail until you can no longer envision the pale.

Because black males are endangered.

Only the lasting,

Unchangeable.

Milk Chocolate

# War At Home

Depression slowly trickling to rage now.

The call of pain getting bogged down.

The forgotten memories of the night terrors rain from the south.

Open wounds, new scars.

Feelings of hurt,

That stain the domestic traits that trails of blood.

Broken trust thrown in the rug.

Hopelessness leaving face,

Trying to keep pace of the taste of blood feeling mouth.

I see, searched for anything.

Things that could stop my domestic intruder.

I fall into the whirlwind,

Protecting those that I can't have hurt.

While the fist creates bruises that protrude through the skin.

The words of a tongue that splits verbs,

The words perks the ears, which cut into cheeks filled with tears.

Hurt more than the impending second blow that will momentary enable you to hear.

It is pain.

Pain that we turn to God and ask for him to explain.

Cursed verses to the Most High.

I can feel your tears filling up now.

How could a brother, sister, uncle, mother, father hurt me?

When all I want is for them to share the love I see.

I love but I will not  let someone under the influence strike me,

But more importantly anyone that I know that won't recover from the blows.

If I could call someone to stop the hurt of the night.

It may be a night...

But that night will be in God's grace.

One day the drunken warrior will see their error.

View the broken bridges and burned towns their drunken breath destroyed now.

And see that they didn't need to do these things.

& the hurt those that loved them through everything.

Keep your heads high to the innocent warriors that try so hard to keep the peace alive.

This is not a normal thing,

But it's happening more common and at an alarming rate.

Just keep faith, and keep as safe as you possibly can.

I will be praying through with you to the end

# America

The build up of generations took apart the humanity of our race.

When I was younger I never could equate black with great.

As a kid they said pick a career, but all the roles occupied had a pale face.

So those couldn't be my dreams.

When the doctors, lawyers and policemen aren't a similar color to me.

Actually nothing in the mainstream media is a color of me.

Unless they are criminals or the athletes.

Where did the hatred come from?

When did black become a lesser trait.

The 300 years of slavery.

Royalty.

Other countries history books tells me I used to be a King.

Battle Royale is the only Royals we ever seen.

Neither will be taught by the books we read.

Lynches were idolized as a glorified count for each town.

They sometimes burned the bodies.

Burned flesh fall down,

As the sweet southern wind whistles through the air with a strange smell.

It's the Black skin.

The skin people think is dangerous,

Already a notion in the head,

That I have to use force first.

Or they may make me dead,

Even if he is an unarmed man.

He is a threat been a threat to white man.

Lethal force is the only reason, to reason to this colored man.

Does he not know what we've done to his color, man?

Is it just my guilt inside that I want to cover in?

Or maybe it's my denial that it happened as severely as everyone has made it seem?

Subconscious racism

Black have opportunities,

Under me.

White Privilege has spoken seniority.

Was food stamps suppose to be our reparation?

Enslave them for a couple 100 dollars a month.

Keep them begging and yearning for the first week of the month.

Kids swelling with hunger,

But our best plan is donate a few meals twice a week.

While we stack meat in the freezer,

Then when it expires we wish we would've found time to eat.

The 6 kids on the other side of town,

Sleeping in the same room would've gave an arm for time to eat.

It all sounds like broken records,

but when this is your life on repeat.

You find moderate comfortable another soul hears your feat.

My feet.

I promise has 10 toes.

I have 10 fingers,

2 eyes.

2 hands.

Why does my color determine if I am a human?

People committing animal cruelty,

Gets jail time.

But the police blasting black kids,

As though being born another color was a crime.

Gets a non conviction,

And paid vacation time.

The media is finally

Exposing the bleeding sore we have living in America.

Some say whites get shot by the police all the time.

True, but did whites ever get lynched by a mob?

Bit by a dog?

Hosed by the man?

Beat by the police that was apart of the clan.

Dragged out their home and beaten because they owed "white" land?

Whites honestly have never felt our pain,

We have been dealt with something worst than any historian can tell.

We are in a land that the law gave it that every man was equal,

But then man was separated by color and that separation spread like a disease .

Black was situated as a color of evil,

White was deemed as pure and good.

They took the complete opposites out of the coloring box.

Selling one higher than the color of charcoal rock.

One higher than the kid with the sagging jeans,

With a hat and a black hoodie.

Walking calming down the sidewalk of the street,

Until a neighborhood watchman decided to reenact the episode of Cops he seen on TV.

Even a white guy with no badge can get away with killing me.

This is the most dangerous place that a black male could be.

Putin is ruthless but I would have a better chance with his country accepting me.

Or maybe North Korea,

They would welcome me.

The Middle East would be a breeze for a guy like me.

I would rather be proclaimed as a known enemy. Then be the baboon they think of me.

# The Difference

Coax into a system that deceives me with rights and
justice,

Just to be shot as I exercise anything I believe.

I guess lady liberty takes naps every time a black child
get killed.

That's why there's unrest because the justice system
gives John a break for shooting Lil Ron.

Lil Ron would've went to prison if he shot John in the
face.

Self defense.

Even with self defense they see a black face.

Precedent was set today.

They don't have to stop,

They will always get away with it.

I think the one thing I need is an apology.

Some kind of heartfelt remorse,

For the black kid in the black hearse.

Some kind of sympathy,

Empathy,

A tear,

Or a poured drink for the homie.

Something.

We came from a relationship of me under you,

I feel like the unaware slave with the Proclamation setting them free.

Then again what is free?

We were never a image painted in this society.

We have to be bolder than the courage we contain,

because being Black there's greatness in your veins.

We have the greatest mind, use it to change the standards today.

Love the skin you are in,

And carry it proud against the American flag that once gave way to oppress your skin,

Blend the pen of injustices of the past to write the new black in history.

With your choice in ink,

Because this is our time.

This is our destiny that King had placed in those many dreams.

God help us not miss the destiny.

As we march to be free but these teens,

Shooting each other in the streets.

It is sad that we march to free,

But most crime that we see with our own eyes is our own kind.

There is a distinct difference between liberty and being free.

Liberty is an external force allowing you to exercise the laws they pass to make you act freely.

But Freedom is a natural process of saying and doing with no external force interfering.

In simple words.

White people have Freedom.

While we just have Liberty.

# Heartbeat II

I wish my heart stopped.

So I wouldn't have to tread my every step.

Watch my every word.

Count my every breath.

I want to make sure the world has surely change,

Before I bloom a beautiful offspring.

With eyes of crème coffee,

Hair of silk curls.

My child will have the energy to fuel a war.

But I would never let a child of mine be drafted into this battle.

Where cowards shoot unarmed mavericks.

Why the weapons?

So many more bullets are produced than possibly needed.

Crime rate declining,

"It is only a matter of time the heroes start becoming the villains."

That was a Dark Knight speaking.

Now as I'm thinking,

I can't protect my kid,

I can't protect myself.

My best protection is to tell him to duck and hid.

Avoid the eyes,

Speak in a whisper,

Detach the all the charisma.

All the charms of right and wrong.

Because as they wrong, your rights are gone.

Then their wrongs get strong as the Justice System plows on to real issues.

Like what gender should be on bathroom doors.

It feels so wrong.

I feel myself detach from me, every time I see a cop around.

How did the badge become the biggest threat?

Aren't they there to protect?

Preserve and enforce the laws created by our elect?

Gangs on the street are more friendly and kind to me.

Unease, I can finally see why my mother and father tried to shield me.

Because their shield will be the only one in my life.

To protect me.

Save me,

Find some kind of salvation in a world that makes you reform your beliefs.

The values you drifted into sleep on.

The American Flag that was once a print on your pillow case, has fallen from it heighten grace.

As Babylon Shakes.

All we can do is wait until we are safe.

# Brimstone

Beautiful brilliance bellowing behind the beast.

Broken brown, brimstone children belching to be free.

Whimsical white kids wishing walls away,

So they can stay within reach of the beautiful brimstone children.

Peachy bleach stained mouths passing personal vows of unity.

But butterflies fly all around the buttery bittersweet cocoon.

Because no one wants to help the trapped once you're free.

Maybe Redirect the regressions of previous regrets and revisit the dimensions of refugees of the west.

Maybe Milky Way stars will tell the difference between deserving and deserted hearts.

Just peeling apart the pickling puzzling heart.

Minds losing matter convulsing patterns of mayhem.

That strays with the lines of kind eyes and soft lies.

This all is confined within the brimstone mind.

As time tapped the beautiful brimstone baffled its kind.

The bleaching of teaching that washed away the brimstones mind.

Now the darker color is whiter than before.

The cream of coffee.

Coke of Cain.

Purity of a slain white lamb.

It's now the Brimstone's day to be Etched into the same.

The beautiful brimstone culture has officially gone away.

Trapping the beautiful brimstone in the cocoon which it lays.

# The Competition of Me

Finish me

Finish free.

Finish first.

I may finish incomplete.

As I describe to delete.

But I provide to defeat the inner anger in me.

Pacifist meets black activist.

Actively working may imply where disaster ends.

Come back and I may just put down the pen!

I had to back out the spotlight.

It was giving me sunburns till the late of night

Making my life less than a black man behind sirens and lights.

I didn't think I would make it through this fight.

With humility and fame, to two mixes like Sprite.

It's bubbly and delicious until you meet your dentist hygienist.

And your seven cavities closes into double digits .

As I fidget and try make a different image.

But it is an image that my labor hasn't been committed.

So what do you want me to do with my list of compliments?

The lines of passion in my head that make room to follow through with all my dark and gloom in my dirty in insanitary lagoon of fools that presumes death but actually moves through in a cocoon of flukes and daisy Dukes that tempts my head to be more sexual than sensual in everything I do!

I may be a man .

But my temptations is something that can kill a man

# Purpose.

Will I ever have worth to work in?

Or boots that work through my ends.

My day raise pay like that day my ancestors realized they no longer were slaves.

Is my chain too tight?

Tight like the belt they put on my jeans from sagging for what I believe?

Do I believe what they say?

Because I can date today but if I date a white girl the date would have to stay out the country and suburban roads because hate is a place that feeds away at gravel and paved roads.

May I eat ?

"Outside , outta sight!"

Sorry that was my 1870's rights.

Still battling the slave complexities to my modern life.

Kites can be flown but only as the strings that keep them low.

Like the lynching of my brothers that trees held up and was a public speculate .

Punish me for my resilience to succeed after centuries of you telling me what my name was going to be.

I will no longer look down on my race and do your racism for free.

I will make sure you take a toll from every exchange you hold in front of me.

When you walk with me through the store you will help me look for everything!

Mr. Manager or Sales Associate directed to keep an eye on me.

But your blind because you can't see how discriminating the act is .

My heavy black skin has been stretch so thin if it was for a few of us,

our minds would've been sucked in.

Centuries of pain and chains that they cleverly mixed with flames and hate would turn any race to believe this is all they would have .

But giving credit on behalf of the slaves my people have made slacks from the cotton we picked and created fabric for the first Black president.

We jumped through the hoops so much in your society we created a Simone Bile's one of the greatest gymnasts that ever lived.

LeBron James, Michael Jordan. Our feats are large,

With scars still lined on our feet.

We bled so much that it began tasting sweet.

We adapted so we could contain the heat.

We all were born from screams but our yelling has never seize.

Cultivating and engulfed with wisdom of the deceased.

Thank you Eugenics, you created the perfect breed.

The Black in and outside of us is your lasting greed.

Wanting to be us ,

so oppression is your squeeze.

But Black culture will never leak for we are strong , stronger than what you believe.

Black Gold the progression of us finally being free.

# Black Boy Privilege

Privileges gifted to me by the States.

1. I'm a black male so white females take a gander to my side. As their eyes wide they fall into the gaze of my darken eyes. I carry the forbidden skin their parents didn't not commend. They wanted a Jake or a Henry. Now they stuck with Xavier and Daquan, with mixed children on their mind. But my Moms got oppressive fear in her heart. She doesn't want us to fall apart and rape charges come up out of spite. Like she has seen happen all throughout her life. Then I get 10 to life and lose the little value of my life.. Black males can get any nationality we need, but it's awesome because our reputation through any race stays as deadbeats.

2. We can make a sound out of anything. Jazz, Hip Hop , Rock we created almost everything. Out of sorrow and pain we can rap through defeat. But with this talent that we speak so many have the gift that it's poison to the black kids to think that's all they have to give. So we all make mixtapes , shape up to labels demands. Dreams of light but reality in the end they are darker then the sky as night begins.

3. We are good at anything we have proper teaching for. Sports are something our 'bodies were just made for'. We must have Mutated genes looking like the Mutant Jean but the Sky is so Gray as we convene on their fields to slave... Oh my bad play. Trap the black kid on sports

for all his life until senior year where even JUCO's won't even  say his name, and now he has no other worth but skills with a ball with no where to play. Isn't that great? I promise you he's fine the Y is open today.

4. We have great chances for Prison. My image makes it a topic that any white person can mention. "Have you been to jail?" No ma'am but I do live in a certain type of hell that every time I excel my skin gets a little tighter as I try to confirm that I'm different than those other males. But no matter the heights I achieve the cops only see the black in me.

5. Cops loves us! Special attention every time we move a muscle. We can be harassed by any action. & if you're lucky you might receive a blast or two that can pass as a hashtag. Even if your just a white man that so happens to make a paper clip badge and play copper as a neighborhood watch dad you can kill me because I am black and it was bound to happen from any one of the gangsters in the trap. At least when you shoot me it will give me some type of fame, a name for myself. And I have you, my skin and racism to thank.

6. Teachers never know what to really do us . Middle age white teacher with so many or few dark skinned students in their chairs with tempers that make their spiky hair flare. Can hardly teach because they can't reach these students that refuse to be institutionalized by learning things that don't pertain to their kind. As little white lies of history lines within the lips of a white teacher. We never are fully engaged and end up never reaching our potential , but wait! We got rap and sports so school is something we don't technically need, so our priorities fail short to behaving worst in classrooms ,

teachers take action too. Pushing students to offices and
the suspension rate for blacks goes through the roof. But
it's a free vacation , totally rad dude.


7. I'm black so I'm obviously cool. The way I talk , the
slang , my walk . Everything I do is the biggest crave
that buzz and rocks, social media. But then we have
appropriations.... that takes all my creations but makes it
more assimilated.

8. I have to prove everything. If I am smart I better be
Einstein at his peak because every word I may think is
combated and evaluated as being wrong. I have to mirror
President Obama, I have to seep greatness in my seat.
Because the line drawn from a black scholar and a
gangster is just a hoodie and some jeans. And if I speak I
am barely heard unless I give someone white my words
and then everyone will jump along. But It is fun like I
am a ghost writer and I am writing all of Drake's songs.
But it has been 400 years this shouldn't last too long.

9. The N word. I can say it , you can't . But it's okay,
now days it's highly contested and frowned upon . By
the time my life gets along the term will be banned
because it is derogatory and it's out of my name even
though back in the slave and modern days it was
acceptable for your race to say it to my face. Now since
time has put restrictions on the word and blacks have
made it cool using it as a noun, adjective , or a verb. The
one privileged word that has been crafted to mock
bigotry,  has been cultural unacceptable by white entities
, but when white people used it, they made it to subject
their rage, but now that it's our term it is just not okay.

They just don't like the limitations, they would never want to TRUMP on a parade . It's just not classy because... well yeah I will wait.

I get so many things. Gee why doesn't everyone want to be black? From extra correction to protection. The Police and Schools love me . The girls come and the expectation is deadbeat. I can be a rapper or athlete. Who needs school? When if go back they will probably suspend me for another week. I have the lowest standards that no one excepts me to even meet. What a great life to be Black in the Land of the free. To be beaten and enslaved and reminded of that constantly. Perceived as a thug even with a college degree. To be pushed to be like Martin Luther King but feel the outrage and pain of Malcolm X's on his darkest day. Black in America the stain of the American Dream every day.

# July 4th.

Barbecues and Fires.

Lighting fireworks in the air with the smoke of patriotism lasting in our lungs.

As we celebrate the day that we won.

Against an oppressive force,

As we impress force against other countries.

I wish we could see how they react when they read we have a 4th of July.

America loves the underdogs,

No wonder they haven't given up.

Because they are altering our playbook.

ISIS may be radicals but so were our patriots.

Why is July 4th a national holiday as it was only freedom from political and economic strains?

But Juneteenth doesn't get a recognizable following for freeing the millions of slaves.

A whole race still surviving today.

Maybe that's why the Indians fought so hard,

Because the heard what brought the white race so far.

So they got inspired,

Picked up their bows and arrows.

As gunpowder shredded through their horses.

But those native warriors could hear the fireworks pouring.

The lights shining and the darkness succumbing.

They could feel freedom in their grasp, if they fought just as the white man had,

For his freedom.

But we don't recognize them as upholders of free countries anymore.

We slap them with names of savages, terrorist threats.

But call ourselves founding fathers.

Word play careful and select.

Why is national security overseas?

As assault rifles are still being concealed to create an internal bleed.

But all the happy families will be doing festivities on July 4th.

I will be doing the same but making sure I'm not to loud and cause a scene.

Or be too black or look to mean.

Or make eye contact to long.

And making sure I pull out my money before I walk into a store.

Because on this freedom day,

This is the only way I can truly enjoy and be safe.

As little kid,

With black patterned to my skin.

Looking out from the shack that they shackled me in.

But there is a small part where the wood slightly breaks.

So I peek out because I feel the shack starting to shake.

Believe it this is my favorite holiday.

I position my bloody feet to give them some rest from the fieldwork of today but still giving me enough room to look both ways.

I can see the brilliant lights flashing.

But limited to the sparks as it starts on the ground.

The excitement and joy those people have as the crowd around.

Dying for the day I can finally see what's above.

The day that my Independence is won.

# Questions...

How many of us is going to have to die for you to see it's not normal?

How many times you times you have to see us cry before you all stop saying something is wrong with us?

How many bullets are we going to have to take?

How many banners we have to make?

How many hashtags we have send before you can finally see, that we hurting?

The Black Community is on flames.

How many names we have to blast before the media picks up the rage?

I am not talking about the looting man.

I'm talking about this emotional pain.

Something so deep centuries of oppression gave it a name.

Cause I'm angry.

How many people you know pay to have someone kill them?

Mm, Zero?

Right...

So give me back my taxes!

Just give me a notice in my mail when the 12 is going to show up so I can have my final meal,

And my family would understand and know it's messed up but they would still have reason to grieve in peace because they know the reason for the slaughtering of me.

Death Row inmates get more humanity than me!

Give me steak, and a priest!

If you know it is going end like Laquan McDonald with 16 shots let me kiss my momma.

Tell her I love her and say only nice things about her.

Say my funeral I want a block party for the whole street,

For little kids to eat for free.

Treat me with some dignity!

A fire squad could be waiting for me, just tell me in advance so I can leave my affairs, and I can die Black peacefully

# I'm getting tired

Of people saying I should more like Martin Luther King

Like the ropes around my brother's neck doesn't give me the right to scream!

To be angry, to seek justice, to be with burdens in my heart.

Breeding farms, auctions, violence, whippings.

Renaming, scraping, killing, raping.

Beating, taming, shaping, and assimilating.

Long divide in history between our two races...

Why do you hate me??

We've fought,

Protested,

Pleaded for equality.

We've been hosed.

Bitten.

Killed for our ethnicity.

So you understand why a little Malcolm X raises up in me.

Why speak for me to be quiet when if I died you would be silent?

Would you cry and mourn with your love for me?

Post my hashtag with the fallen black soldier's body count climbing causally!

I'm not Militia because I speak my Black Actively!

I'm actually more patriotic than white supremacist could ever be!

Because it's not just my movement, it's my movement of minorities!

We don't want to kill no white peoples.

We love all the peoples.

We just want things a lot more equal.

I cannot stop dialogue about racial issues because it feels uncomfortable.

Because stopping it allows it to never exist in the classroom.

Recycling racist thoughts and rhetoric to be hatch.

Tainting another generation with inequality on their backs.

So Equal protection should be granted even though our land is good to where put your keystone pipeline.

Free At Last! For Standing Rock!

Free At Last!  For immigrants' rights!

Free At Last! For my Muslim family.

Free At Last! For all of my African American communities.

Free At Last! For all my minorities living in oppression!

Thank God almighty one day we will all be Free At Last!

# If I was White.

Literally if my skin redden to the touch or turned purple when squeezed too much.

If I was white, I would smile.

The world is my platter and I can sample how I choose.

Rules and laws gets ambiguous the more I make.

I would run,

Jump in lions dens that fight to the nearing of death till the siren comes on saying the game is over.

Doing it just for the fear that could be created within my soul.

What a thrill!

Because I'm white,

I'm invisible or invincible whatever I decide.

I am me,

I could sing drunk, sing along, sing in front it would be my song.

My wings would flap from the early of days to the Dawns of nights.

Then I would simply walk home,

Greeting the officer and telling him to have a great night because I'm white.

Every cop is my friend, they can get me out of tricky jams or traffic jams with escorts to work or play.

I'm white I'm never afraid!

Maybe if minorities acted more like me these banners for live wouldn't be a need.

It would be something more tasteful like All Lives Matter,

It's safe and simple and we can all get behind it and gather

## In White

Sympathize with others

Love the differences

Grow within cultures

# Something I've Noticed

Something I've noticed is the way people do not hesitate
to pretend terrible things haven't happened
But                                              Maybe
It's less acting and more defending
We're afraid that if we accept that there's a problem then
we will be forced to try to change
Because as we all know the first way to fixing a problem
is accepting you have one
So listen to this issue that is worldwide
People do not love people
People are afraid
People are hurt
And angry and tired
We are all so tired of turning the page to tomorrow and
finding another horror story tragedy there
We are writing history books of hate
And I always believed that this age would one day be
considered the time of great change or invention
But as more days pass I find that this age is the time of
hate and ignorance and lack of peace
Because peace has become an ideal
It is unrealistic
Impossible is the first word associated with tranquility
We have forgotten that every individual has some reason
to live whether it be a lover or a mother sister or little
brother
Everyone has some reason
Yet we have a tendency to put our lives first
No second empathetic thought of those who may have the
same want to live as we do
We are breaking
Humanity is shattering

And we are brushing the shards beneath the crust we walk upon without second thought
We forget that those pieces are just like us
Just like we will be if we do not begin to change
Because we all make up this broken Earth
It is not just the children shooting other children at war
It is not just the oppressed minorities we pretend we're not trying to ignore
It is not just the high school children breaking under the pressures of test scores
Because a 20,000 dollar debt rate after graduation is considered a small price to pay for an an education we are required to have to have a chance at happiness one day
It is not just the hands outstretched on street corners with begging fingers trembling
It is not just the mentally ill shrinking themselves to nothingness
No we all make up the broken
Because how can there be any healthy souls when there is this much broken piling at our feet
No
We are all drowning or tripping or digging our ways out of the piles and piles of the dreams we have all taken part in taking away

# Blue

Sometimes I believe that you built the sky for me

Placing each piece carefully because if you moved to quickly it would collapse

And again

I'd be left with nothing but darkness where blue should be

But how can I be so helpless

So dependent

There are children living through bombs that rip their families to shreds

Their fingers clasped and knees bent on dirt

Eyes praying to the sky

To God. To Allah. To God.

Asking for peace.

Asking for strength to keep hoping

Asking for these days to fade

Into nothing more than memories

Into crumpled pages in history

Into nothing more than an ache in the knee when the rain falls onto quiet homes

Their skies are filled with so much more than blue

They are filled with dust and tears and prayers for a world where peace comes before greed and hate and anger

Their skies are filled with hopes so full they're spilling onto the ground onto their battered feet

Their skies are filled with so much more than blue

And they are crumbling

But these people

These strong glorious warriors of hope

Hold what they can on their shaking shoulders

In the hopes that someone will come

And help them simply by taking their hand and telling them their fight is not for nothing because peace is on its way

And it's bringing thousands of backs

Who will help them put the sky back where it belongs

## Humans

And as the world fell asleep

The sun lost its grip on the sky and the clouds clawed at
her fingertips

But she fell anyway

And every night

The moon shrinks herself more and more as if she wasn't
already small enough in a galaxy that stretches on
without end

And she cries shooting stars onto the earth below

The universe is just as human as we are

**"White privilege"**


White

Gold

I am white with skin that blares "this person has a future with promise"

I am white-first generation American

British mother with Canadian father with white grandparents from Kenya

I am white with a family I do not have to fear of losing to a government that steals the joy from families in the middle of the night and scrapes their bodies up chimneys on Christmas Eve not caring if pieces of them were left behind

I am privileged.

Do not tell me that white privilege does not exist when I know first-hand it does

Because my best friend and I are both first generation Americans

But she cannot pass through airport security without setting off every prejudiced alarm within the hard wired brains of white security guards

They see

"Brown" "terrorist" "Muslim" "Isis" "bomb"

They do not see "person"
"feelings""beliefs""faith""love"

Do not tell me that my ability to walk through TSA pre check and not even have to take off my shoes is not privileged

Do not tell me you are not privileged when you do not have images of being torn from your mother's shaky hands as you are sent back to a foreign land you have never known yet they say it's where you belong -

Every time you see a police car

You do not understand, nor will you ever have to

Because you are privileged

But listen.

Privilege does not make you a better or worse person than you really are

Just like the skin of my best friend- you did not choose it

You did not choose to be born into this world where we wear our skin like battle flags

Splitting us into teams and tearing into one another without remembering that underneath us are all the same color

We are all red and pink and bloody

We do not have to rip off the skin of each other to find that

Because it's already been proven true

During the civil war, the holocaust, the trail of tears,

Why are people so cruel to people because our skin doesn't match

We are constantly playing chess

But for the longest time the white pieces on the board have captured and enslaved their opposition

But this is not a game

People are not a game

Our lives are not a game

White privilege exists. Just accept that. It's okay.

Its okay

But it's not okay

How is it okay that I am given opportunities that others aren't solely because of genes I didn't choose?

I want opportunities because I worked for them

I want opportunities because I deserved them

But now I must live with heaviness in my heart knowing that my closest friends will always be viewed as below me

Less than me

Not as worthy as me

Solely because the skin we were born into doesn't fit quite right into this country's view of who deserves what

And my heart is heavy

It weighs down my fists clenched screaming for love

We must love

Where can we find the white hands, fingers, clasping
brown hands holding peace?

Where can we find a quiet place where fears are quiet?

And I swear

Nothing will ever sound as heavy as the fear in my
aunt's voice when she called my uncle to say goodbye

You see she lives in South Africa

She knows it is unsafe, but it is her home

And one night as the sun dipped below the tree line her
car died

And she knew it wouldn't be long before they found her
and took advantage of a woman alone at twilight

So she called my uncle voice heavier than the weight in
her still beating heart she said goodbye

Knowing that her chances of living were slimmer than
her chances of seeing the sun again

That. Is what fear sounds like.

Yet I hear voices filled with fear as heavy as lead
speaking about fists that are not the same color as theirs,
they fear, not the fist, but the skin around it

But what is there to fear other than the images media
have created to put fear in our hearts about hands

Why are we scared of hands?

Hands create art and brush away tears

Hands hold each other

But hands also hold the guns aimed at the product of racial discrimination

Hands have created walls to separate people who were different

But we must remember

Hands are not the enemy

We do not have to be enemies

Because our hands can intertwine.

And we can stand and say

No more

## Skin in Protest

It appears the English language requires more definition

Apparently the word "no"

Has begun to become lost in translation from gritted teeth to ear

Because no is ignored and passed like a stop sign on a quiet country road

Hell, the question isn't even asked

Lips and tongue and teeth don't even have a chance to move

To shape

A one syllable word

"No" that we bite down on like the bullet between shivering teeth

Leaving silence

So we are forced to use the only language that may still be understood

We freeze

We close our eyes and pray that if we hope hard enough our skin will become as cold and sharp as icicles on a frozen winter day

That our bones will become the peaks of mountains pushing through our silk skin

I'm white I'm never afraid!

Maybe if minorities acted more like me these banners for live wouldn't be a need.

It would be something more tasteful like All Lives Matter,

It's safe and simple and we can all get behind it and gather

# If I was White.

Literally if my skin redden to the touch or turned purple when squeezed too much.

If I was white, I would smile.

The world is my platter and I can sample how I choose.

Rules and laws gets ambiguous the more I make.

I would run,

Jump in lions dens that fight to the nearing of death till the siren comes on saying the game is over.

Doing it just for the fear that could be created within my soul.

What a thrill!

Because I'm white,

I'm invisible or invincible whatever I decide.

I am me,

I could sing drunk, sing along, sing in front it would be my song.

My wings would flap from the early of days to the Dawns of nights.

Then I would simply walk home,

Greeting the officer and telling him to have a great night because I'm white.

Every cop is my friend, they can get me out of tricky jams or traffic jams with escorts to work or play.

Since our lips are not given the chance to say no

Let our bodies do the talking

Since apparently all it takes is a piece of flesh to mean yes

Even when every other part of our skin prickles with protest

# The Nameless

Recently, I've been flattered with the compliment from several people

That they are inspired by my constant positivity

That they admire the way I smile in the face of

"All of what you've been through"

And although this makes my heart soar

I need people to know that

What "I'm going through"

Is nothing compared to the silent wars waging in the hearts of others around me

What I'm going through

Is nothing

It's just louder

More obvious

What I'm going through does not deserve a Purple Heart because my heart is still intact inside my chest

There are others next to me whose homes are as shattered as the mug that hit the tile floor as their mother answered the phone

There are others who have cried so hard they didn't think their eyes would still be able to see if they happened to open them the next morning

My battle. Is nothing but a water gun fight?

Because I have waves of people on my side

The smiles we should praise are not mine,

But the ones on the faces of people who are going through this fight alone

They may have water balloons and water guns strapped to their chest but they only have two arms

And two hands

And one heart

They cannot make it in a world that is against them

Then need fingers to clench in protest

Standing up for them when they have stood up for themselves for far too long in a world where we barely glance in their direction

# I Am

I am a white girl

I am every shade of privilege an American can be born into

Except for the fact that

I am a woman

And even though that is not a minority

Society still somehow manages to shrink us into bite-sized "less important" pieces

I am a white girl

And a feminist, and a "black lives matter" supporter, and an ally of the LGBTQ community, and a voice of the undocumented citizens who deserve to just be called *people*,

I am an advocate for humans and their equality

Because that's what all of these movements really mean

You see

I am a white girl

Who lives in America?

I am a white girl

Who is ashamed to call herself American?

Who has wanted peace since she was too young to even know what sort of wars were waging around her?

Who has since realized the only way to find peace in a world that weans on hate?

Is to make sure my voice is heard above the violent cacophony of ignorance and misunderstanding

I am a white girl

And I am aware that how much I care about inequalities that do not directly affect me

Will make people uncomfortable

And that is okay

Because I am aware that how much I care is unusual

And I will not allow it to overshadow the voices of those who have felt these oppressions I speak of first hand

Because I have only watched it and felt it

Through the veins and throbbing hearts of those who I care about most

I have never felt the sting of an unfair system prick my skin to prove that I actually matter

My accomplishments have never been shaved down to my skin color

So I will stand by those who have

# Let it Out

Stop.

Breathe in.

Let it out.

I want you to close your eyes and let the anxiety of yesterday today and tomorrow fall away

Let yourself stand shivering and bare

You are stripped of all weighing you down

You are free

Stop.

Open your eyes and look where you are

Where you are right now

Wiggle your toes and clench your fists

Scrunch your nose and blow the clouds a kiss

You are alive

More than that

You are living

I don't know when this world decided punishment was necessary for mistakes

Or who decided what was a mistake and what was learning

But the truth is they are synonymous

Do not let the black holes of the failures of yesterday

Suck you in

Keep going.

Because did you know that black holes are the absences
of all light, and they will drag down any photon they can
get

Be bright

Be greater than all the Suns in this galaxy

Because you are greater than the Milky Way

No matter what you have done in the past you are so
much more than that

You are great.

Be a knight in shining armor

And this world the castle you're about to seize

You are unbreakable

Be the fire in the dragon's belly

You are unquenchable

And honey

You add up to be so much greater than the mistakes of
your past

You are so much more perfect

Than a set of numbers and tests

This system is incapable of measuring the amount of beauty you hold within

# Stand

I stand with you

No

I do not know your hardship

I do not know the feeling of your future constantly dangling by strings of who the hell knows what will happen next

I do not know the feeling of being granted this brilliant right of being acknowledged as a person in the United States after years of believing you had already been one

But the government likes to hold it over your head that you're not

I do not know the feeling of going to the hospital to be treated even though it could mean losing your home and being sent back to place you have never really called your own but it's where you acquired your beautiful skin and accent that makes the "real" Americans swoon

It's where your mother was born and raised and you are proud to call yourself Latino even though all she wants is for you to call yourself Americano

So you do

You do your best

You push yourself to be the greatest you can be for her

"Undocumented immigrants in America"

May I please just call you hermano, mejor amigo, mi igual

Fuerte y valiente

Because that is what you are

You are person, human, friend

You are not papers or green cards or numbers

You are no less than those of us who were lucky enough to be born here

You are my equal

And I will not stop fighting for you until that is true

# Too Close to Home

Black man shot by police

Black man shot

Man shot

Man

May we take hands bow our heads and pray

May we take hands and pray

Take hands and pray

Take hands

Pray

We pick and choose what Is important to us

We find the words that affect us most

We listen only to the pieces we want to hear

We can't listen to too much

Only the pieces we can chew

Don't bite off too much

Or else you may actually be compelled to do something

To change something

Man was shot in Tulsa

Too close to home

It's only an hour away from where my safe feet stand

I am up in arms

Because everywhere is too close to home

Every life taken out of fear from generalizations

Is another story

Another Facebook fight

Another argument

Why do we feel the need to correct each other

When

Man was shot

Father was shot

Son was shot

Daughter was shot

Husband wife mother sister brother cousin
granddaughter

Was lost

Lost

Fingers slipped out of time

Hands we can't hold any more

Stories only heavy in our hearts anymore

People have been lost

Over and over

Out of anger

Fear

And confusion

All lumped together in headlines and hashtags

It won't be long before #blacklivesmatter #racialdiscrimination #treyvonmartin

#*insert name here*

Is all we have left?

Everywhere is too close to home.

People matter no matter how many miles away their fingers slipped away from their families shaking hands

People matter how dark their fingers are

People matter no matter how afraid we are of what they COULD do

People matter

People

Man

Hands

Pray

Please. Stop taking away the pieces that matter to you

And start taking away pieces that matter to us

To all of us

To hands that can hold each other up

No more deaths

No more too close to home's

No more brothers and sisters lost

May we be able to inhale together

And exhale

And be okay

Together.

**In Black In White**

Love

    Worship

        Unity

**Become the humans you would want your children to be**

# Foreigner

When she turns nine she learned about the 9 planets that orbit in the same galaxy as the place she called home

At 10 she tried tried to find which planet she was supposed to have come from because it was definitely not this one

At 11 she decides it's probably Pluto

At 12 Pluto no longer is a true planet and she's even more sure that's where she belongs

Because she has a whirling atmosphere that she thought would draw people in but rather it pushes them further out

Her Gravity is surpassed by others misunderstanding

She has eyes like all 5 of Pluto's moons, they're almost bigger than she is- and they will take in every pieces of this Earth she doesn't believe she belongs in

People believe she has unbreathable air

But it's only because they have been to scared to take a breath

She is capable of sustaining life

The people around her just need to believe

She's just as brilliant as the Milky Way, you just have to really take her in

She could be a galaxy of her own

If you let her

She may think she is from Pluto

But in truth

Her gravity is like the sun

She feels she doesn't belong because she is keeping the planets from falling off their axes

She is quietly holding the world together

Don't let her atmosphere or her Milky Way eyes keep you out

Because her core is brighter than you could ever imagine

# Heart Beater

He sees the heart and savors after its taste.

Maybe he no longer has a beat.

Days are thrown wrapped around sweet words and verbs
like the coil of a Boa Constrictor's squeeze.

She pleads for his words to be true,

But he is lukewarm in a pool of goo.

Trying to make feelings that seem warm.

Meaning swimming through his head but can never
make the words blend to the blood that rushes to his
head when he sees he cannot love you like you can.

You are captivated by his words.

He promised the things you seen in your story books
with pictures and shiny covers.

You took him in your hand and felt his arms and knew
he could secure you.

Love.

Pure hearts love easily like a faucet.

Once turned on the rushing falls instantly.

But him with damaged pieces,

Things rusting his pipe line and creating cracks that
discolors the water like Rio Green.

His water is lumpy.

Is it his fault or hers?

He is pained every time he sees a heart he's hurt.

It's like being burned and try to find the best burn cream to subdue the pain.

He needs someone to fill the flames and gaps he lost in the past.

But his heart creaks like an old door on rusty hinges

If she wants to get in,

She's going to have climb through the haunted house of his rib cage

Past ghosts of heartbreaks past

And over the arteries that are afraid to beat for anyone but himself

Because his heavy door heart can't afford to be opened to just anyone

She has to be more than just the other half of his heart

But she has to be a whole one

Strong enough to support the heaviness his holds without hesitation

She has to be the power of the ocean

Strong enough to come back every time she gets pushed away

She will not mind being his everything.

## Exist ft Chy and Kayleigh Peters

Have you ever thought about your existential existence?

What if Heaven came to Earth for a visit?

Minutes ticking time and space conflicting with supernatural beings and morals eating on top of Mount Olympus.

Perfection opposed to chaotic and jumpy souls showing the product of the fallen angel's goals.

Wings tearing flesh,

Kevlar feeling anointed bombs

There is no lines of lies that judgment day could ever find.

I guess human beings aren't ready to face the divine.

As the sun shine,

We find comfort in Angel's eyes.

But they turn and run as they don't see a trace of God in our minds.

Battle torn,

Swore as men and women prepare for the last instances of war.

Breathing in intelligence exhaling peculiar petulance.

Time for fighting to be released.

God v Humanity.

Creation going outside the reams to defeat their design intentions.

A reach that will be in a moral depiction of the human wholes.

Would we believe it was God if he actually came down?

Or would we believe it was just another judgements soul?

Constantly shifting our thought in an attempt to help

Feeling the embrace of heaven somehow turn into hell.

Still feigning for an acceptance into those golden gates

Our burning flesh hoping to be cooled by that supernatural embrace.

Inability...

Inability to find what it takes to win the jury over.

How to convince the crowd without having to wishing upon a three leaf clover.

The inability to capture the meaning of it all

Things like "without this figure called 'God' could I still stand tall"?

Things like "I know about Adam and Eve, but not too far from the tree does the apple fall"

Your existential existence...

Tell me do you think about it?

You think you know who you are with prayer, but please question who you would be without it.

Your reason combatting with the books of the Bible.

From Genesis to Revelations; each one equally significant to your survival.

Oh yes, but what if?

Sitting lonely in your space wondering if true religion is more than a brand or a stitch.

Thinking that maybe you'll get a sign or a hint.

Only death after life, these thoughts running through our minds.

Hoping for something that proves the divine.

Some sort of unsaid law that's spoken without word

Something that moves you so potently it's nearly said to be absurd.

Comfort... it is the reason we are content. But God makes it clear he is the reason we exist.

Hypocrisy at its finest sashaying to church alters •

Proclaiming to be a Christian but speak hatred amongst Gods followers.

The size of a mustard seed they say about faith is enough

You must feel it not see it to believe it,

But sometimes situations will call that bluff

Tasting on your tongue the sting of disbelief

Scorching your mouth with the ice of controversy

But the real question is where does it end?

your existential existence, or the divinity of Gods plan?

# Untitled 1

My want flies for you as a feather of an eagle flowing easily through the wind.

As it plummets to the earth I can see gravity tilting the gentle feather to the ground but some how I still enjoy the descend.

I have journeyed the bellows of the earth but the touch of you has gained the curiosity of my heart to define my yearn for you .

Sometimes the air gets so tense with anticipation when I see you , if I sneezed it would feel as though I would break it .

I want you.

So much that it concaves at the ends of my mouth that my cheeks start to burn red when I speak of you.

When I hear your name the syllables stop and play a tune in my heart that makes me inflame with passion behind others claim to speak of you.

You are mi amor, the rose, the Sky.

If you ever departed,

my heart would create quakes that shakes as the earth making an escape from my fury and wrath to find the tracks that you last had.

Adoring you will forever be my task.

**I've felt the world.**

Heard her screams.

Felt loneliness and how the fear comes as she leaves.

I love you.

Love even though the seasons were harsh and at times we forgot each other's names.

My love has only grew, hidden in the flames.

I felt days where my passion was dark.

I wish words could truly express feelings.

My heartbeat had been without rhythm.

Honey bunches without sweetener.

I am a patient without a doctor.

A Lover without a partner.

I am sick without the only girl that makes me want to work harder.

So I will fight for her until my heart gets lighter, and her words gets sharper and my image gets smaller.

I will forge keys for her till the deep night.

Write letters till they become typed.

My Care can never Leave as I Hope to complete my promises and hopes in those ancient dreams.

# About the Authors

Kayleigh Peters is a student at Oklahoma City University. She is a Cellular Molecular Biology major and hopes to minor in both French and English. Kayleigh began strongly pursuing her love of writing in her 11th grade creative writing class with Mrs. Cherith Ferguson at Harding Charter Prep High School. She began by writing free-verse poetry, which quickly became her passion, but also learned to work with structured prompts and styles as well as short stories. Spoken word poets have also had a strong impact on her writing, and have led her to write more openly about experiences in her own life. Kayleigh strives to impact people's lives with her writing the way her favorite poets impacted her, while inspiring others the way the people in her life have inspired her.

Gregory Samuel is a senior at Harding Fine Arts Academy. This is currently his third book published . He has a passion for people and is looking forward to college to pursue a degree in Political Science and Business. Gregory Samuel started his poetry at a camp called KAA that cultivates young Christians to follow their desire for God. With this growth he continued to write and soon became noticed at school, organizations, publishers and news outlets for his incredible use of words and his amazing speaking skills. Gregory strives to influence and empower the world with his words and to create a new depiction of the African American male.

97498929R00052

Made in the USA
Lexington, KY
30 August 2018